What Muhammad Said About JESUS

ALI SHAWKAT

KENANGA PERMAI

Published by

Kenanga Permai Sdn. Bhd. (554903-T)
Unit B1-07, PJ Industrial Park,
Jalan Kemajuan, 46200 Petaling Jaya,
Selangor Darul Ehsan, Malaysia.
Tel.   : 603-7956 4127
Fax.   : 603-7958 1943
E-mail : *mail@kenangapermai.com.my*
Visit our website at *www.kenangapermai.com.my*

Copyright © Ali Shawkat 2006, 2015
Design © Kenanga Permai Sdn. Bhd 2006, 2015

All rights reserved. No part of this book may be reproduced in any form or by any means without prior permission from the publisher.

ISBN 978-983-2965-19-0

Printed in Malaysia

Contents

INTRODUCTION	1
CHAPTER 1 *BIRTH AND LIFE OF JESUS*	7
CHAPTER 2 *PHYSICAL FEATURES*	17
CHAPTER 3 *SECOND COMING OF JESUS*	20
CHAPTER 4 *JESUS ON THE DAY OF JUDGMENT*	33
CHAPTER 5 *VIRTUES OF JESUS AND MARY*	45
CHAPTER 6 *MUHAMMAD'S CONNECTION TO JESUS*	51
CHAPTER 7 *THREE NARRATIONS FROM THE COMPANIONS OF MUHAMMAD*	54
GLOSSARY	67

Introduction

JESUS IS A UNIQUE FIGURE IN HUMAN history. His words and deeds inspire many, and his life continues to fascinate and raise questions. So, it comes as no surprise that Muhammad, the Prophet of Islam, would mention him. But what might surprise many is how often Jesus is mentioned, and what Muhammad had to say about him. This book collects these sayings in an attempt to understand the place of Jesus and Mary in Islam from the mouth of Muhammad himself.

The range of these sayings takes us through the pivotal moments in Jesus' life, from his birth to the end of time. We witness the virtue of Mary and the Immaculate Birth, and get a glimpse of Jesus' ministry and the critical moments before his rise to the heavens, then are told of Jesus' Second Coming, and end with Jesus as a key figure in events on the Day of Judgment. All of this with such attention to details as to describe the looks of Jesus and what he will be wearing on his second visit to earth. Jesus emerges from these sayings as an important religious and historic personality, with great significance for the future.

The importance of this topic stems from one of the major dilemmas facing our world today: How do we understand a religion or a religious community that is not our own, and how can we escape the trap of emotional judgments and stereotypes, and cut through layers of suspicion to reach the truth? Much of the friction between religions today is fuelled by historical and contemporary misunderstandings, further complicated by religious, political, and economic rivalries; the misunderstandings obscure reality, while the rivalries breed unjust treatment of others. And it is only through the pursuit of truth and justice that we can ever have hope of bringing peace to this earth. It is puzzling how many of us in the world today demand justice yet fail to be just, and how much we struggle for acceptance and understanding yet fail to accept others.

If we accept the maxim that we should treat others as we would like to be treated, then we should understand them as we would like them to understand us, and be fair to them as we would like that they be fair to us. So, to truly understand a religion we ought to hear what it says about itself in its own words, not what others say about it. Then proceed to judge it, if we were to judge, with standards that we don't mind applying to ourselves. Thus is the importance of presenting the actual sayings of Muhammad in this book.

Since these sayings address a host of issues, the book discusses several important beliefs in Islam and includes relevant verses from the Quran, the Muslim scripture, for further elaboration. Whenever the Quran is quoted, its verses are in italics, followed by brackets that include the chapter and verse number. The glossary serves as a quick guide of key terms discussed in this book. It is hoped that this book will not only offer its reader a better understanding of the place of Jesus and Mary in Islam, but also a richer understanding of the Muslim faith in general.

This book collects thirty sayings of Muhammad and three sayings of his companions, arranged in seven chapters with some commentary. The format followed here resembles what can be found in classic *Hadeeth* books.

What is a "Hadeeth"?

A *Hadeeth* or *Hadeeths* (pl.) is Arabic for what Muhammad said and did. It is considered part of what God revealed to Muhammad, and its importance cannot be understated in all aspects of Muslim life.

What follows, and is indented, is a brief background of Hadeeth. If it is found to be too technical, the reader can comfortably skim over it, as it is not essential to the rest of the book.

Short history of Hadeeth

When Muhammad said or did something, it got reported to the person who did not witness it through a middleman, or a narrator. Then that person reported to it another, and so on. Hence, each Hadeeth came with its own set or chain of narrators.

Then, each Hadeeth was examined based on the reliability and credibility of its narrators. If all the narrators were found to be of good character and memory, then the Hadeeth would be accepted as an authentic report of Muhammad. But if a flaw were found in the narrators, the Hadeeth would be labeled as weak.

Are there any weak Hadeeths in this book?

Only authentic Hadeeths have been included in this book, and the weak ones have been excluded. The last chapter has three sayings from two of the companions of Muhammad, which are not technically Hadeeths, but they will be referred to as such in this book for the sake of simplicity. The chain of narrators, which usually accompanies every Hadeeth, has been omitted entirely for the sake of simplicity too.

Why only authentic Hadeeths?

Weak Hadeeths are not reliable and cannot be attributed with certainty to Muhammad. What is attributed to Muhammad is valid only if it is authentic. This is a point worthy of remembering when reading Islamic literature, as many fail to make the distinction between authentic and non-authentic Hadeeths. If the Hadeeth is unreliable, Muslims usually do not follow it.

Where do I find Hadeeths?

The words and deeds of Muhammad, or Hadeeth, are collected in countless volumes and arranged in a variety of ways. There are six main Hadeeth books, but by no means do they exhaust all of the sayings and actions of Muhammad. The most famous of them are *Saheeh al-Bukhaari* and *Saheeh Muslim*.

What does a Hadeeth book look like?

Hadeeths are often arranged in chapters and sections under specific headings, and some authors add commentary to them.

How does this book resemble a classic Hadeeth text?

This book arranges Hadeeths in seven chapters, with commentary that follows each one. Thus, the reader will get a taste of what it feels like to go through a classic book of Hadeeth.

Chapter 1
Birth and Life of Jesus

1. **"All the children of Adam are touched by the devil when they are born, except for Mary and her son."**[1]

   - This Hadeeth is from *Saheeh Muslim*, one of the most important books of Hadeeth, in a chapter titled, "The virtues of Jesus, peace be upon him."

   - When Mary's mother was pregnant with her, she prayed to God, *"I seek refuge with You for her and her children from Satan"* (Quran 3:36-37), and God accepted her prayer and protected Mary and Jesus from the touch of the devil. Other Hadeeths add that the devil pokes the side of every new born with his finger, and so the child cries when it is born. But when Satan went to do so with Jesus, there was a barrier that Satan could not break.[2] This is a clear virtue for Mary and

Jesus, peace be upon them. Implicit in this divine protection from the devil and his influence is the confirmation of the chastity of Mary and the Immaculate Conception, which the Quran explicitly confirms (3:45-48; 19:16-33). God further protected Jesus by saving him from those who wanted to kill him; see Hadeeth (30) and commentary on Hadeeth (5).

2. "God ordered John son of Zechariah to observe five commands and to order the children of Israel to observe them. Then it is as if he procrastinated, so God revealed to Jesus, 'Either he conveys them or you do.' So Jesus went to John and said, 'You were ordered to observe five commands and to order the children of Israel to observe them. So, either you convey them or I do.' So John said, 'O spirit of God, I fear that if you do it before me that I would be punished or that the earth would collapse under me.' So John gathered the children of Israel in the Jerusalem Mosque until it was full and he sat on the balcony, and he thanked God and praised Him and then said, 'Indeed God ordered me to observe five commands and to order you to observe them. (1) The first is that you worship God and take no partners with Him. For the one who takes a partner with God is like a man who buys a slave with his own money, with gold or silver, then gives him a house to live in and says, 'Work and give back to me.' So the slave works and gives to someone other than his master. So, which of you would like his slave to be like that! And God is the One who created you and provided for you, so worship Him and take no partners with Him. (2) And I order you to pray. And when you stand to pray, do not turn your faces away, for God faces his servant when he prays as long as he does not turn away. (3) And I order you to fast. For fasting is like one who has a bundle of musk in a company of men, and all of them love its smell. And indeed the smell of the fasting person is sweeter to God than the smell of musk. (4) And I order you to give charity. For charity is like one who was captured by the enemy, and they tied his hands to his neck and were about to kill him, so he said to them, 'Can I ransom myself from you?' And he paid and paid until he freed himself. (5) And I order you to remember God often. For it is like one whom the enemy was fast after, then he came to a fortress and took refuge in it and saved himself. And so the servant of God does not protect himself from the devil except through the remembrance of God.' "[3]

- We see here the interaction between two prophets of God, Jesus and John, peace be upon them both. We also are witnesses to John's sermon in Jerusalem and how popular it was; the Mosque was full to capacity or beyond. The word *mosque* in Arabic means *place of prostration*, and refers to the place where God is worshipped. All the places the prophets built for worship are considered mosques. Prophet Muhammad, peace be upon him, said, "The first mosque to be established on earth was the Sacred Mosque in Mecca, and then the Mosque in Jerusalem, and the time between them was forty years."[4]

- It is clear here that prophets receive revelations from God, and are under His watch and correction. So, as moral examples and trustees of God's message, it is impossible for them to commit moral crimes.

- The Quran describes Jesus as a spirit from God (4:171), and here too he is addressed as such. Jesus is unique in that he was conceived without a father, but instead the angel blew the spirit of Jesus into Mary. And it is because of this that Jesus is referred to as a spirit from God or the spirit of God, the latter an honorific title. Such honorary names abound in the Quran, e.g. *the house of God* (2:125). Also, a camel was dubbed *the camel of God* in the Quran (7:73) when it miraculously appeared from a mountain with no parents, given as a sign to one of the prophets. It is understood that the camel is not divine, and the house of God is obviously not divine. Similarly, the *spirit of God* or *spirit from God* does not indicate divinity.

- The parable John presents in the first command seeks the closest example humanly possible to God's extreme bounty on His servants and how much they owe Him. God's favor upon people requires that they worship Him alone, and not give part of that worship to any other.

3. "Jesus son of Mary saw a man stealing, so he said, 'Did you steal?' The man answered, 'No, by He whom no one else deserves to be worshipped except Him!' So Jesus said, 'I believe in God and deny my eyes.' "[5]

   - This is a testament to Jesus' piety. God was so great in the eyes of Jesus that he would deny what he saw with his own eyes if someone swore by God to the contrary.

4. "The scripture of Abraham was revealed on the first night of the month of Ramadan. And the Torah was revealed after six days had passed from Ramadan. And the Gospel was revealed after thirteen days had passed from Ramadan. And the Psalms was revealed after eighteen days had passed from Ramadan. And the Quran was revealed after twenty four days had passed from Ramadan."[6]

   - Ramadan is the month of fasting for Muslims, and it was in it that the prophets received their sacred books. This signals the commonality between the messages of the prophets, as God chose to reveal their books in the same month despite the centuries and millennia separating them. It also signals the virtue of Ramadan as a sacred month from days of old.

5. "The roof of my house was opened when I was in Mecca and Gabriel descended and opened my chest and washed it with water from the well of Zamzam in Mecca. Then he brought a golden basin filled with faith and wisdom, and emptied it in my chest, and then he sealed it. Then he took me by my hand and lifted me to the lowest sky. And when we came to the lowest sky, Gabriel said to the gatekeeper of the lowest sky, 'Open.' He asked, 'Who is this?' He answered, 'This is Gabriel.' He asked, 'Do you have anyone with you?' He answered, 'Yes, Muhammad is with me.' He asked, 'And he received the call to be a messenger?' He answered, 'Yes, so open.' Then, when we ascended the lowest sky there was a man with a crowd to his left and a crowd to his right. When he looks to his right he smiles, and when he looks to his left he cries. Then he said, 'Welcome O righteous prophet and righteous son.' I asked, 'O Gabriel, who

is this?' He answered, 'This is Adam. And the crowds to his right and left are the spirits of his children. The crowd on the right is the people of heaven, and the crowd on the left is the people of Hellfire. So, when he looks to his right he smiles, and when he looks to his left he cries.' Then Gabriel lifted me until he came to the second sky, and he said to its gatekeeper, 'Open.' And its gatekeeper repeated what the gatekeeper of the lowest heaven said, then he opened the gate. Then I passed by Enoch and he said, 'Welcome O righteous prophet and righteous brother.' So I asked, 'Who is this?' And he answered, 'It is Enoch.' Then I passed by Moses and he said, 'Welcome O righteous prophet and righteous brother.' So I asked, 'Who is this?' And he answered, 'It is Moses.' Then I passed by Jesus and he said, 'Welcome O righteous prophet and righteous brother.' So I asked, 'Who is this?' And he answered, 'It is Jesus son of Mary.' Then I passed by Abraham and he said, 'Welcome O righteous prophet and righteous son.' So I asked, 'Who is this?' And he answered, 'It is Abraham.' Then I was raised to a place where I could hear the creaking of the pens. And God obligated on my nation fifty prayers. So, I returned with that until I passed by Moses, and he asked me, 'What did your Lord obligate on your nation?' I answered, 'He obligated fifty prayers.' Then Moses said to me, 'Ask your Lord to reconsider, for your nation will not be able to bear it.' So, I returned to my Lord, and He took away half of them. Then I returned to Moses and told him, and he said, 'Ask your Lord to reconsider, for your nation will not bear it.' So I returned to my Lord and He said, 'They are five (in number) but they are fifty (in reward). My Word does not change.' Then I returned to Moses and he said, 'Ask your Lord to reconsider.' But then I said, 'I feel shy of my Lord.' Then I was taken until I came to the Tree of Outmost Boundary, and its fruits are like the great jars of Hajar and its leaves are like elephant ears, the leaf could cover this nation. Then it was covered with indescribable colors. Then I was admitted into paradise, and I found in it domes of pearls and its sand was from musk.'"[7]

- In this ascension, we see several of the renowned prophets of God, beginning with Adam and ending with Abraham, peace be upon them all. Another Hadeeth mentions Prophet Muhammad praying on the same night in the Jerusalem Mosque,[8] and meeting other prophets such as Abraham, Moses and Jesus, whom he lead in prayer.[9]

- Jesus is unique among the prophets mentioned here in that he is the only one who is still alive. The Quran denies that Jesus was killed or crucified, but rather he was lifted alive to the upper skies to save him from his enemies (4:157-158). And he remains there alive till today until he comes back to earth (4:159; 43:61). See also Chapter 3 in this book.

- The creaking pens are those of the angels copying God's revelation and destiny of all creatures. The Tree of Outmost Boundary marks the end point, where whatever is ascending to God is received and beyond which the knowledge of all creatures ends.

- Heaven's soil is from a beautiful smelling musk and its houses are pearls. Prophet Muhammad described heaven as having "what no eye has seen, and no ear has heard, and no human heart has imagined."[10]

Chapter 2
Physical Features

6. "I dreamt last night that I was at the Ka'bah in Mecca, and I saw a dark-skinned man, with the most beautiful skin of men you could see. He had long straight hair to his shoulders, as the most beautiful hair you could see; and he had combed it, and it was dripping with water. And he was reclining on two men, and circling The House in worship. So, I asked, "Who is he?" And I was told, "The Messiah son of Mary." Then I saw a man with frizzy hair, and a defective right eye as if it is a grape extinguished of light. And I asked, "Who is he?" And I was told, "The Imposter Messiah.' "[11]

- The stark difference in the physical features of Jesus and the Imposter Messiah highlights the stark difference between their respective messages. Jesus will be calling to the worship of the One True God as a prophet of God, while the Imposter will call himself God and call to his own worship. The beauty of the message of Jesus corresponds to his physical beauty, and the unseemly appearance of the Imposter testifies to the deformity of his message and falsehood of his claims. Prophet Muhammad said, "No prophet was sent except that he warned his people about the lying one-eyed Imposter. Indeed he is one-eyed, and your Lord, the Most High, is not one-eyed. And between the Imposter's two eyes is written, "Disbeliever."[12] In another statement, Prophet Muhammad said, "I have spoken to you so often about the Imposter until I have hoped you would comprehend. The Imposter Messiah is a short, bowlegged, frizzy haired man, with a defective eye that is flat with his face, not bulged or dented. But if you are confused, then know that your Lord is not one-eyed."[13] The appearance of the Imposter is evidence that he is not God, because the Imposter is blind in one eye. Even if you are confused and forget what I told you about him, Prophet Muhammad said, at least know that God is perfect and safe from any deformity, and so the Imposter cannot be your Lord.

Physical Features

- Jesus is described here as dark skinned, and Hadeeth (9) describes him as reddish white. This means that his skin tone is in-between these colors; he is lighter than black and darker than white, with visible redness. This moderation in color is similar to his moderation in height; he is neither tall nor short. His hair is straight and reaches to his shoulders. He is also described as having a broad chest.[14]

- The Ka'bah is the cubic structure in Mecca, the site of the first place of worship on earth.

Chapter 3
Second Coming of Jesus

7. "The Hour will not come until ten signs come to pass: the sun rising from the West; the Imposter; the Smoke; the Animal; Gog and Magog; the coming of Jesus son of Mary; and three earthquakes: one in the east, one in the west, and one in the Arabian Peninsula; and a fire that will come out from Eden and drive the people to the Gathering Place."[15]

   - These major signs foretell the chaos and upheaval that is to come on the Day of Judgment. The second coming of Jesus is one of the major signs that the Day of Judgment is near.

   - The Animal will come out towards the end of time and talk to people because of their lack of faith (27:82), and the Gathering Place is greater Syria.

8. "I swear by the One who has my soul in His Hand, The Son of Mary is about to descend in your midst as a just ruler. And he will break the cross and kill the swine and stop accepting the religious tribute. And wealth will be so abundant that no one will take it. And a single prostration in worship would be better than this world and what is on it."[16]

- Jesus will descend as a just ruler and he will rule with Islam. As Prophet Muhammad is the last prophet, the message and legislations he brought are final. Jesus, peace be upon him, will come down to enforce and follow them.

- When Jesus descends, he will remove any confusion and declare that he is neither God nor the son of God. Once this happens, and with the power and victory that God will give to him, Christianity will come to a natural end. All people will follow Jesus and will become Muslims. And thus there will be no separate religious communities to pay the religious tribute.

- Wealth will be abundant because the earth will be blessed at that time, and people will not pursue worldly gains out of their piety and knowledge that the Day of Judgment is very near.

9. "The prophets are like stepbrothers: they have different mothers but their religion is one. And I am the closest human to Jesus son of Mary, since there was no prophet between him and me. And he will descend; so when you see him, recognize him. He is a man of medium height, closer to a reddish white complexion, dressed in two light yellow garments, as if his head is dripping with water though it is not wet. And he will fight people for Islam, break the cross, kill the swine, stop the religious tribute, and God will end in his time all religions except for Islam, and kill the Imposter Messiah. And peace will be put on earth, so that the lions will graze with the camels, and the tigers with the cows, and the wolves with the sheep; and children will play with snakes but the snakes will not hurt them. And Jesus will stay on earth for forty years, then he will die, and the Muslims will offer the funeral prayer for him."[17]

- The message of all the prophets is essentially the same, and only particular laws differ from one to another. For that reason, the prophets are like stepbrothers because they have so much in common, with the backbone of their messages identical.

- Killing the swine means prohibiting its consumption and ownership, and allowing its killing.

10. "It is not The Imposter that I fear most for you. If he comes out while I am among you, I will be his opponent on behalf of all of you. But if he comes out while I am not among you, then each one is responsible for himself, and God is the caretaker of every Muslim on my behalf. He is a man with extremely frizzy hair, and a protruding eye; he looks like Abdul-Ozza ibn Outn. So, whoever meets him should read before him the opening verses of the chapter: The Cave (18:1-10). He is going to come out between Syria and Iraq, and will spread mischief to the right and to the left, so be strong O servants of Allah." We asked, "O Messenger of God, how long will he stay on earth?" He answered, "Forty days: a day like a year, a day like a month, a day like a week, and the rest of the days are like your regular days." We asked, "O Messenger of God, in the day that is like a year, is the prayer of a regular day sufficient for us?" He answered, "No. Give it its due portion." We asked, "O Messenger of God, how fast will he be on earth?" He answered, "Like the cloud driven by the wind. He would come to a people and call them to accept him, and they would believe in him and obey him, then he would command the sky and it would rain, and would command the earth and it would be green, and their cattle would come back to them fat and full of milk. And he would come to a people and call them to accept him, but they would reject his call, so he would leave them and they would suffer a drought and become destitute. And he would pass by a ruin and would say to it, 'Bring out your treasures,' and its treasures would follow him like swarms of bees. And he would call a man brimming with youth and would strike him with the sword into two pieces that get separated the distance between the archer and his target, then he would call him and the man would come laughing with a happy face. Then God will send Jesus son of Mary, and he will descend at the white minaret east of Damascus, wearing two saffron-dyed garments, placing his hands on the wings of two angels. If he lowers his head, it drip's, and if he lifts it up water rolls from it like pearls. And it is not possible for a non-believer to find the smell of Jesus and remain alive, and his smell extends to where his vision does. Then he will look for the Imposter until he finds him at the door of Ludd and will kill him. Then Jesus son of Mary will come to a people that God has protected from the Imposter, and he will wipe over their faces and tell them about their stations in paradise. Then God will reveal to Jesus, 'I have brought out servants of mine that no one has the power to fight, so shelter my servants in the Mount of Toor.' And God will send out Gog and Magog, and they will swarm down from every hill. And their first would pass by the lake Tiberias and drink from it, and their last would pass by it and say, 'Once there was water here!' And the

Prophet of God, Jesus peace be upon him, and his companions would be so besieged that the head of an ox would be worth more to them than a hundred pieces of gold for you today. Then the Prophet of God, Jesus, and his companions will pray to God, and God will send on Gog and Magog worms in their necks and they all will die at once. Then the Prophet of God, Jesus, and his companions will come down from the mount and find no place on earth except that was filled with their rot and stench. Then the Prophet of God, Jesus, and his companions will pray to God, and God will send birds with necks like camels, and they will carry them and dump them wherever God wishes. And Muslims will light fires from their bows and arrows and quivers for seven years. And God will send a rain that no city or desert house can shelter from, and it will wash the earth and leave it spotless like a mirror. Then the earth will be told, 'Bring out your fruits and restore your blessings.' And it is then that the group of people will eat from the pomegranate and seek shade under its skin. And milk will be blessed; the small camel's milk would be enough for a large group of people, and the small cow's milk would be enough for a tribe, and the small sheep's milk would be enough for a group of relatives. Then God will send a sweet wind, and it will come to them from under their armpits and take the soul of every believer and every Muslim, and only the wicked people will remain. They will fornicate in public like donkeys, and it is upon them that The Hour will rise."[18]

- The Imposter will come first and claim that he is God. He will be blind in the right eye, with the left bulging out. The power that he will be given will be a great test for people, to see who will stay firm on the true faith or will worship the Imposter.

- The Imposter represents the height of the mortal claim to divinity, and it is only fitting that Jesus would be the one to kill him.

11. "The Imposter will come out in my nation and stay for forty. Then God will send Jesus son of Mary, as if he is Orwah son of Mas'ood al-Thaqafi, and he will seek the Imposter and kill him. Then people will stay for seven years with no animosity between any two. Then God will send a cool wind from the direction of Syria, and no one with the slightest of faith in his heart would remain but the wind would take his soul, so much so that even if one of you were to go into a mountain, it would go after him till it takes his soul. And the wicked will remain; light as birds in flight to evil, and with the morals of predatory animals, they know no good and forbid no evil. And Satan will appear to them and say, 'Will you respond?' And they will say, 'What do you command us?' So he commands them to worship idols and they will worship them, during which they will be in abundance of provisions and comfort of living. Then the Horn will be blown, and no one would hear it except would turn his head to it. And the first who will hear it is one who is fixing the water reservoir of his camels, and he will fall dead and people will fall dead. Then God will send rain like a drizzle, and people's bodies will grow because of it. And then the Horn will be blown again, and people will be standing and looking and waiting. Then it will be said, 'O people, come to your Lord, *'and stop them, they will be questioned.* (37:24)' Then it will be said, 'Bring out the portion of the Fire from people.' It will be asked, 'How many?' And the answer will be, 'From every thousand, nine hundred and ninety nine.' That is the day when children will grow gray, and that is the day when the Leg will be uncovered."[19]

- The percentage of people going to Heaven is one in a thousand. Another Hadeeth adds that upon hearing this, the companions of Muhammad were worried and asked Prophet Muhammad, "Which of us will be that one that will be saved?" So, he answered, "Be happy! The nine hundred and ninety nine will come from Gog and Magog, and the one (going to heaven) will come from you. By the One who has my soul in His Hand, I hope that you will comprise one quarter of the people of Heaven. I hope you will comprise one third of the people of Heaven."[20]

- Children will go gray because of the great difficulty and turmoil of the Day of Judgment. God warns people of the Day of Judgment and asks them to prepare themselves for it, *"O people, obey your Lord. Indeed the earthquake of the Hour is something terrible. On the day when you will see it, every nursing mother will abandon what she nurses, and every pregnant woman will abort her pregnancy, and you will see people as if they are intoxicated, yet they are not intoxicated; but the punishment of God is severe"* (22:1-2). The only way to be saved from this difficulty is through obeying God, *"Then if you disbelieve, how will you save yourselves from the Day that will make children go gray"* (73:17). Consult the following chapter for more on this.

- God blesses with wealth, and He also sends it as punishment. Many people assume that as long as they are wealthy and healthy that God is pleased with them. But in Hadeeth (10), Jesus and the believers go through hardship and poverty, yet that does not mean that God hates them. And the idol worshippers will be wealthy and comfortable, yet that does not mean that God loves them. Wealth and health are not sufficient indicators in themselves of God's love.

12. "Two groups of my nation God has protected from The Fire: a group that opens the land of al-Hind, and a group that will be with Jesus son of Mary."[21]

- Refer back to Hadeeth (10) for the tests the companions of Jesus will go through and their virtue. There is a clear exhortation here for the pious to support and keep the company of Jesus, peace be upon him, when he comes back.

13. "What a sweet living it will be after the descent of Christ! What a sweet living it will be after the descent of Christ! The sky will be permitted to rain, and the earth will be permitted to grow plants, so that even if you were to sow your seed on a solid smooth rock, it would grow. And there will be no greed and no envy and no hatred, so that one will pass by a lion and it will not hurt him, and would step on a snake and it will not harm him. There will be no greed, no envy, and no hatred."[22]

- This will be an unprecedented period in human history. After great trials, the righteousness of the people is rewarded with these great blessings. All people will worship God and follow His religion, and for that the blessings of earth will multiply.

14. "By the One who has my soul in His Hand, the son of Mary will embark on Hajj or Omrah or both of them at the path of al-Rawhaa'."[23]

- Hajj and Omrah are rituals associated with the Sacred House in Mecca. When Jesus comes back, he will participate in that worship and visit Mecca, which signifies that he will follow the religion of Islam. Other prophets have performed this pilgrimage too, as Prophet Muhammad said when he was on his way to Mecca, "As if I can still see Moses peace be upon him coming down from that hill, raising his voice with the chant of pilgrimage. As if I can still see Jonah son of Amittai peace be upon him on a red compact camel, dressed in wool, and the bridle of his camel is from palm-tree fiber, repeating the chant of pilgrimage."[24]

Chapter 4
Jesus on the Day of Judgment

15. "I am the master of all people on the Day of Resurrection, and do you know why? God will gather all people, their first and their last, on one plain ground where the call can be heard by them all and the eye can see them all; and the sun will draw so close to them that they will be in distress that they cannot bear. So, the people will say to each other, 'Don't you see what state you're in? Won't you seek one who could intercede before your Lord?' Then they will say to each other, 'Seek Adam.' And they will come to Adam and say, 'You are the father of all humans, and God created you with His Hand and blew in you from His spirit and ordered the angels to prostrate to you and taught you the names of everything. Intercede for us before your Lord! Don't you see what we are in? Don't you see

what we have become?' And Adam will say to them, 'My Lord is angry today like He was never angry before and will never be angry after. And he forbade me the tree, but I disobeyed Him and committed a sin that brought me down to earth.' And he feels shy from His Lord the Most High. 'Myself, myself, myself! Go to someone else, go to Noah.' So they go to Noah and say, 'O Noah, you are the first messenger to Earth, and God had called you a thankful servant. Intercede for us before your Lord! Don't you see what we are in? Don't you see what we have become?' So Noah will say to them, 'My Lord is angry today like He was never angry before and will never be angry after. And I had a prayer that I used against my people.' And he feels shy from His Lord the Most High. 'Myself, myself, myself! Go to someone else, go to Abraham.' So they will go to Abraham and say, 'O Abraham, you are the Prophet of God and the Close Friend of God from the people of the earth, so intercede for us before your Lord. Don't you see what we are in?' So he will say, 'My Lord is angry today like He was never angry before and will never be

Jesus on the Day of Judgment

angry after. And I told three lies.' All these lies he used to defend the religion of God. And he feels shy from His Lord the Most High. 'Myself, myself, myself! Go to someone else, go to Moses whom God spoke to and gave the Torah to.' So they will go to Moses and say, 'O Moses, you are the Messenger of God. God has favored you with His message and Speech over people. Intercede for us before your Lord! Don't you see what we are in?' So he will say, 'My Lord is angry today like He was never angry before and will never be angry after. And I killed a human I was not allowed to kill.' 'And he feels shy from His Lord the Most High. 'Myself, myself, myself! Go to someone else, go to Jesus, the servant of God and His messenger and His word and His spirit, who used to heal the blind and leper and raise the dead.' So they will go to Jesus and say, 'O Jesus, you are the Messenger of God and His word that He sent to Mary and a spirit from Him; and you spoke to people in infancy. Intercede for us before your Lord. Don't you see what we are in?' So Jesus will say, 'My Lord is angry today like He was never angry before and will never be angry after. I was worshipped instead of God. Myself, myself, myself! Go to someone else, go to Muhammad peace and blessings be upon him, the master of the children of Adam and the first to be resurrected from earth, a servant whom God has forgiven his past and future sins.' So they will come to Muhammad peace and blessings be upon him and say, 'O Muhammad, you are the Messenger of God and the last of the prophets, and your past and future sins have been forgiven. Intercede for us before your Lord. Don't you see what we are in?' So I proceed and come under the throne and I prostrate to my Lord. Then God favors me with beautiful praises of His which He gave to no one before. Then it will be said, 'O Muhammad, raise your head. Ask, and you will be given. And intercede and your intercession will be accepted.' So I raise my head and say, 'O my Lord, my nation, my nation!' So it will be said, 'O Muhammad, admit into paradise those who will not be held accountable from your nation from the right gate of the gates of Heaven, and your nation will share the other gates with the other nations.' And by the One who has my soul in His hand, the width of the gate is like the distance between Mecca and Hujar (city in eastern Arabia), and as the distance between Mecca and Bosra (city in Syria)."[25] "Then I intercede, and I will be given a group that I will admit into paradise. Then I will go to God a second time, and when I see Him I will prostrate, and He will leave me as long as He wants to leave me, then will say, 'Rise Muhammad. Speak and it will be heard, ask and it will be given, and intercede and it will be accepted.' So I praise him with praises He teaches me. Then I intercede, and a group will be given to me and I will admit them into paradise. Then I will go a third time and when I see my Lord the Blessed and Most High I will prostrate, and He will leave me as long as He wants to leave me, then will say, 'Rise Muhammad. Speak and it will be heard, ask and it will be given, and intercede and it will be accepted.' So when I raise my head I praise him with praises He teaches me. Then I intercede, and a group will be given to me and I will admit them into paradise. Then I will go a fourth time and say, 'O Lord, the ones left inside Hellfire are the ones held back by the pronouncement of the Quran.' So, whoever said, 'There is no one worthy of worship except God' and had the like of one grain of barley of good in his heart will leave Hellfire. Then whoever said, 'There is no one worthy of worship except God' and had the like of one grain of wheat of good in his heart will leave Hellfire. Then whoever said, 'There is no one worthy of worship except God' and had the like of the smallest good in his heart will leave Hellfire."[26]

- The excuses that the prophets, peace be upon them, gave not to intercede were either things that God has forgiven, as with Adam, or were not sins at all. Yet their extreme fear of and respect for God, and the severity of the Last Day, prevents them from assuming the position of the intercessor. Prophet Muhammad, peace be upon him, is the only one to be promised that position.

- What is referred to here as the lies of Abraham can hardly be called lies. Prophet Muhammad said, "Abraham, peace be upon him, did not lie except for three lies: two of them for the sake of God, when he said, *'I am sick,'* (37:89) and when he said, *'This biggest idol among them did it,'* (21:63). And when he was with (his wife) Sarah and they came upon a tyrant, and the tyrant was told, 'There is a man here with the most beautiful woman.' So, he sent for Abraham and asked him, 'Who is she?' and Abraham replied, 'My sister.' Then Abraham came back to Sarah and said, 'Sarah, there are no believers in this land except for me and you. And he asked me about you and I said you were my sister, so don't belie me.' Then the tyrant sent for her, and when she came he went to touch her with his hand and he was attacked by a seizure. So he said, 'Pray for me and will not harm you.' So she did and he was released from it. Then he went to touch her again and he was seized like the first time or harsher. So he said, 'Pray for me and I will not harm you.' So she did and he was released from it. Then he called one of his chamberlains and said, 'You did not send me a human! You sent me a devil!' And he gave her Hagar as a servant. Then she returned to Abraham while he was standing in prayer, and he signaled with his hand, 'What happened?' She replied, 'God foiled the plot of the disbeliever and gave Hagar as a servant."[27]

- The part about Prophet Muhammad's intercession is abbreviated in this specific Hadeeth in confidence that the omitted part will be understood. The intended meaning is that Prophet Muhammad intervenes to ask God to judge people and relieve them of the long wait, and God accepts his intercession. Then, Prophet Muhammad will ask God to save his nation when God starts judging all people.

- The ones left in Hellfire by the prouncement of the Quran are those who disbelieved in God and took partners in worship with Him. God says in the Quran, *"Indeed God does not forgive that partners be taken with Him, and He forgives everything else to whomever He wishes"* (4:48). God, the Most Merciful, will admit into Paradise the one who has the tiniest of good in his heart, as long as he worshipped God alone. This is, in essence, the religion of Islam, which all the prophets of God called to. Hence, all the prophets of God were Muslims, inviting people to Islam. And that is why Islam, in that sense, is the only religion that God approves of and accepts, *"And whoever seeks a religion other than Islam will not have it accepted from him, and will be among the losers in the Hereafter"* (3:85).

16. "God will gather the first and the last for the appointed known day, and their eyes will stare at the sky for forty years waiting for the judgment. And God will descend on clouds from the Throne to the Chair, then a caller will say, 'Would it not satisfy you from your Lord, who created you and provided for you and commanded you to worship Him and take no partners with Him, that He would join each people with what they used to seek and worship in the world? Isn't this just from your Lord?' And they will say, 'Yes.' Then they will go, and the form of what they used to worship will appear to them. So, some will go after the sun, and some will go after the moon, and some after the idols. And the devil of Jesus will take the form of Jesus to those who used to worship Jesus, and the devil of Ezra will take the form of Ezra to those who used to worship Ezra. And Muhammad and his nation will remain, so the Lord will appear to them and come to them and say, 'Why don't you move as the people have moved?' And they will say, 'There is a sign between us and Him, and when we see Him, we will know

Him.' And God will say, 'What is it?' And they will say, 'He uncovers His Leg.' And it is then that God uncovers His Leg and they prostrate for Him. And there will be some people who want to prostrate but they cannot, their backs will be like cattle horns. Then God will say, 'Raise you heads.' And He will give them light in proportion to their deeds, and the Lord will be ahead of them."[28]

- The devil is the one who calls to the worship of other than God. Therefore, anyone who worships other than God is in fact obeying and worshipping the devil. That is why the devil will take the shape of Jesus and Ezra for those who used to worship them, and lead them into Hellfire.

- The attributes of God do not resemble those of His creation. God hears and sees, becomes angry and pleased, but all that does not mean that He is human-like. God is unique in how He looks and acts. The similarity between God and us stops at the name and description, whereas the reality is completely different. The Leg of God is one of His attributes that are beyond our comprehension and imagination, and no one should understand from it that it looks like a human leg. It is clearly stated in the Quran that nothing resembles God, *"There is nothing like unto Him"* (42:11).

- The Day of Resurrection will be covered in darkness, and the only available light will be the one God gives to people in proportion to their faith and good deeds. This light is what will help each find their way to Heaven.

17. **"Jesus will be fed his defense. God will instruct him when He will ask, *'And when God will say, 'O Jesus son of Mary, did you say to the people, 'Worship me and my mother instead of God?'* (4:116). So God will direct him to say, *'Glory be to you! It is not for me to say what I have no right to say. If I had said it, You would have known it. You know what is hidden in myself and I do not know what is in Yours. Indeed, You are the Knower of the unseen'* (4:116)."**[29]

- This exchange between God and Jesus will take place on the Day of Judgment. Its purpose it to honor Jesus by clearing his name and announcing his innocence from any false belief that was attributed to him. It will also serve as reprimand for anyone who worshipped Jesus or his mother, as they will see the ones whom they worshipped denouncing that same worship and any claim to divinity.

- Those who were worshipping Jesus, or any other pious righteous person, were not doing that in obedience to them. Jesus, like any righteous person, calls only to the worship of the One God, affirming at the same time their own mortality and servitude to the Lord.

Chapter 5
Virtues of Jesus and Mary

18. "The best of the women of the world are: Mary the daughter of Imran, Khadeejah the daughter of Khuwailed, Faatimah the daughter of Muhammad, and Aasia the wife of Pharaoh."[30]

- Faatimah is the daughter of Prophet Muhammad, and Khadeejah is his wife. Aasia is Pharaoh's wife, and she is mentioned in the Quran (66:11). This Hadeeth honors Mary as one of the best four women of the world.

19. "The Prophet, peace and blessings be upon him, called Faatimah on the day of The Opening of Mecca and spoke to her in secret, and she cried. Then he spoke to her and she smiled. Then when the Prophet died, I asked her about the reason of her cry and smile, and she said, 'The Prophet, peace and blessings

be upon him, told me that he is going to die, so I cried. Then he told me that I am the best of the women of paradise, except for Mary the daughter of Imran, and I smiled.' "[31]

- Mary is proclaimed to be the best woman who has ever lived. There is a whole chapter in the Quran, chapter 19, which carries her name and tells her story and speaks of her virtue.

20. "Al-Hasan and al-Husayn are the best of the young men of paradise, except for the two cousins, Jesus son of Mary and John son of Zechariah. And Faatimah is the best of the women of paradise, except for Mary daughter of Imran."[32]

- Al-Hasan and al-Husayn are the grandchildren of Prophet Muhammad. Despite their virtue, John and Jesus are better than them. God chose His most beloved to be His prophets, and both John and Jesus were righteous prophets of God. A prophet is one who receives revelation from God through Angel Gabriel, and it is the highest position any human can reach. It should be noted that there are no more prophets after Prophet Muhammad, peace be upon him.

Virtues of Jesus and Mary

21. "Whoever would be pleased to look at the humility of Jesus, should look at Abu Thar."[33]

- Abu Thar is a famous companion of Prophet Muhammad. He was known for his humility and rejection of worldly excesses; he was also known for his truthfulness, such as the Prophet said, "The sky did not shade, and the earth did not carry one of truer speech than Abu Thar."[34] Abu Thar's control of his worldly desires, along with his humility and soft heartedness, resembles that of Jesus, yet it is understood that it can never match it.

22. "If God were to hold me and the son of Mary responsible (i.e. not forgive us) for what these two have done – the thumb and the index finger – He would punish us and would not be unjust."[35]

- This shows God's extreme mercy in that if He were to hold two of his most beloved prophets responsible for only what two of their fingers have done, they would deserve punishment. So, no one stands blameless before God, but it is God who forgives and pardons.

- No matter how much good one does and how much faith one has, it is God's mercy that saves from Hell. No amount of good done is adequate thanks for God's blessings or a worthy price for Heaven. Yet the way God's Mercy is earned is through good deeds; good deeds are necessary to enter heaven, but are not sufficient in themselves. This is like someone who wants to buy a house but does not have the money. So, a generous rich person promises to gift him most of the amount if he can only secure the down payment. The man works and collects the down payment, and sure enough, the rich person keeps his word and pays the rest, and the house is purchased. That man cannot claim that his money bought the house, but yet it was indispensable for its purchase.

23. "Do not exaggerate in my praise as the Christians have exaggerated the praise of Jesus son of Mary, but instead say, the servant of God and His messenger."[36]

- Exaggerating the praise of Jesus is by calling him God or the son of God, worshipping him, or giving him divine qualities. There is a difference between loving someone, and giving him the

Virtues of Jesus and Mary 49

qualities of God. If we were to imagine that Jesus is on earth right now, those whom Jesus would love and call his own would be the ones that believe and follow his message. And the message of Jesus and the words that he left behind do not include a call to his own worship or a claim of divinity; these were things that were said about him but not by him. There is no greater disobedience of Jesus than to contradict his message and worship him with God. And Jesus would surely reject those who say that they love him, yet still continue to disobey him.

- Love, of any kind, can induce exaggerations and extremes that can come back to destroy the love that created them. Guarding against the extreme is guarding love itself.

- Both Prophet Muhammad and Prophet Jesus, peace be upon them, are two extraordinary individuals, but are still humans and are still servants of God.

24. "Whoever testifies that there is no one worthy of worship except God alone, without any partner; and that Muhammad is His servant and messenger; and that Jesus is His servant

and messenger, and the son of His female servant, and His word which He sent to Mary, and a spirit from Him; and that Heaven is true; and that Hell is true; and that the resurrection is true; God would admit him into paradise, according the his deeds, from any of the eight gates of heaven he desires."[37]

- This is a comprehensive statement of creed, and that is why the one who firmly believes in it will have his pick of any of the eight gates of Heaven to enter from. The first statement affirms divinity and the right of worship to God alone, and negates both to any other. The second affirms that Muhammad is a prophet, but does not exaggerate his status beyond that of a human and a servant of God. And the same status is given to Jesus. Affirming the humanity of Jesus is opposite to mistaking him as God or the son of God, or worshipping him. And affirming that Jesus is a prophet is opposite to calling him a magician, a liar, or just a sage. The part about Mary declares her humanity, and affirms the Immaculate Conception, clearing her from allegations of adultery. The last part affirms the reality of Heaven, Hell, and the Last Day when people will rise from their graves and stand for judgment before God.

Chapter 6
Muhammad's Connection to Jesus

25. "I am the (fulfillment of) the prayer of my father, Abraham. And Jesus son of Mary, peace be upon him, was the last to give the good news of my coming."[38]

- The prayer of Prophet Abraham, peace be upon him, was, *"Our Lord, and send to them a messenger from them, who will recite to them Your verses and teach them the Book and wisdom and purify them. Indeed You are the Mighty, the Wise"* (2:129). Prophet Muhammad was the fulfillment of this prayer and the mercy that God sent to all humanity, *"Say (O Muhammad), 'O people, I am the messenger of God to you all, from the One who has dominion over the heavens and the earth"* (7:158), *"And We have not sent you (O Muhammad) except as mercy to all beings"* (21:107).

- Each prophet prepared his people for the next prophet to come, and Jesus was no exception. He was the last prophet to foretell the coming of Prophet Muhammad and command people to follow him. *"And remember when Jesus, son of Mary, said, 'O Children of Israel, I am the messenger of God confirming the Torah that came before me, and bringing good news of a messenger that will come after me, whose name shall be Ahmad"* (61:6). Ahmad is another name of Prophet Muhammad.

26. "God has taken the covenant from me as He has taken the covenant from the prophets; and Jesus son of Mary gave glad tidings of me. And my mother saw that a light came out of her and lit the palaces of Syria."[39]

- The covenant from the prophets is to deliver the message that God has entrusted them with. See also Hadeeth (29).

- The light shining upon Syria is the guidance of Islam spreading to the land of the prophets.

27. "If any of you meets Jesus son of Mary, let him convey to him my *salam* (greeting)."[40]

Muhammad's Connection to Jesus

- Muslims are entrusted to remember to deliver this greeting to Prophet Jesus, peace be upon him. The warm feelings between the two prophets are a result of the love that each has for the other as a fellow believer and prophet. The prophets of God are like real brothers to each other. See Hadeeth (9).

28. "The one who believes in Jesus and believes in me shall have two rewards."[41]

- Each person receives a reward from God for the good that they do, and God's reward is immense. But to receive double the reward is truly to be favored. The one who believes in Jesus then believes in Muhammad has believed in two prophets and two revealed books from God, and so gets double the reward for his faith and courage. See also Hadeeth (31).

- Believing in one prophet naturally requires believing in the next, since the latter prophet confirms and does not contradict the message of the former, while the former has left his people clear signs that tell about the next prophet. For signs of Muhammad in the Bible, please consult *Muhammad in the Bible*, by Abdul Ahad Dawud.

Chapter 7

Three Narrations from the Companions of Muhammad

29. "In explaining the Saying of God, the Majestic and Exalted-'*And when God extracted the offspring of the children of Adam from their backs*' (7:172)-he said, 'God gathered them and He put them in pairs. Then gave them form and asked them to speak, and they spoke. And He took the covenant and pledge from them-'*and made them witnesses over themselves. He said, 'Am I not your Lord?' They answered, 'We testify You are.'* (7:172)- God said, 'So, I make the seven heavens and the seven earths witnesses over you, and I make your father Adam a witness, so that you do not say on the Day of Resurrection, 'We did not know about this.' Know that there is no one to be worshipped but Me, and there is no god but Me, and do not take any partners with Me. I am going to send you my

messengers to remind you of My pledge and covenant, and will send you My books.' They said, 'We testify that You are the One we worship and You are our God, and we worship no one but You.' And they accepted it. Then Adam, peace be upon him, was raised above them to look at them, and he saw the rich and the poor, and the beautiful and the one who is not. He said, 'O Lord, why haven't you made your servants equal?' God said, 'I love to be thanked." And Adam saw the prophets, as if there were lamps inside them, with light shining from them. And the prophets were specified for another covenant: the covenant of prophethood and messengership. And this is God's saying, the Blessed and Most High, *'And We took from the prophets their covenant, and We took it from you (Muhammad), and from Noah, Abraham, Moses, and Jesus son of Mary'* (33:7). Jesus was among those souls and God sent him to Mary, peace be upon them both, and he entered from her mouth."[42]

- God gathered all the souls and they willingly testified that God is their Lord. The belief in God is anchored in every soul and is part of its makeup, thus it finds itself naturally inclined to it. Each one is born with this pure nature that knows God, and only due to influences of upbringing and worldly desires does this get covered up until it can hardly be recognized. But no matter how deeply buried it might be, the soul will never be truly content until it reconnects with its Maker. God reminds us that belief is our true heritage and free choice. Though we have no recollection of this event, the messengers and revealed books remind us of it, and the believers accept it as the truth that their souls testify to. God has established enough proofs in the created world that point towards Him, that after deep contemplation, one can come to the same firm conclusion that his soul had reached before.

- God has varied his bounties to be thanked. When the rich see the poor, they thank God for what they have. And when the poor see the rich, they realize the burden and corrosive effects of wealth in this world, and the accountability for it on the Day of Judgment in how it was earned and spent, and so they thank God. When the healthy see the sick, they thank God. And when the sick see how heedless of God the healthy are, they thank God. Each realizes that no matter what God has given them or withheld from them, there is always good in what God does.

- Jesus was a soul like all the rest, and was carried to Mary by the angel, and the soul entered into Mary from her mouth.

30. "When God wanted to raise Jesus to the heavens, Jesus came out to his companions, and there were twelve men of the disciples in the house, and he came out from next to a spring in the house with his head dripping with water, and he said, 'There are some of you who will deny me twelve times after they have believed in me.' Then he said, 'Which of you volunteers to have my image put on him and be killed in my place and be with me in paradise?' And a man from among the youngest there stood up, but Jesus said to him, 'Sit down.' The he repeated the request and the man again stood up, but Jesus said, 'Sit down.' Then he repeated the request and the man again stood up and said, 'I will,' and Jesus said, 'You are him.' So the image of Jesus was put on him, and Jesus was raised from a hole in the roof of the house to the

heavens. And the search party came from the Jews, and they took Jesus' double and killed him and crucified him. And some of them denied Jesus twelve times after believing in him. And they divided into three groups. A group said, 'God was among us, as long as He wished, then He ascended to heaven,' and these are the Jacobites. And a group said, 'The son of God was among us as long as he wished, then God raised him to Him.' And these are the Nestorites. And a group said, 'The servant and messenger of God was among us as along as He wished, then God raised him to Him.' And these are the Muslims. So, the two disbelieving parties united against the Muslim one and killed them, and Islam continued to be hidden until God sent Muhammad, peace and blessings be upon him."[43]

- The crucifixion here is a story of sacrifice, not of betrayal. The young disciple accepted the likeness of Jesus and was killed in his place, and Jesus was saved. The disciples were privy to this, and the truth made it out and was espoused by a group that believed Jesus to be a prophet of God. Yet, subsequent persecutions almost wiped them out. See the next Hadeeth.

- The division after Jesus into three groups and the example of the Jacobites and Nestorites are an explanation of the confusion and bitter dispute that ravaged the early Christians. The disagreement over the nature of Jesus and how to reconcile a claim of divinity with humanity continues until today among Christian sects. When Islam came, it removed the confusion by clarifying that God does not mix with His creation, and the only one who is divine is God; everything else is created.

31. **"There were kings after Jesus son of Mary, peace and blessings be upon him, that had changed the Torah and the Gospel. And it was said to the kings, 'There is no insult greater than what these people are insulting us with, for they read, '*And those who do not rule by what God has revealed are indeed the disbelievers*, (5:44)' in addition to what else they fault us with when they read. So summon them, and have them read as we read and believe as we believe.' So the king summoned them and gathered them, and**

gave them a choice between death and abandoning the reading of the Torah and the Gospel except for the parts that they altered from them. So they said, 'Why do you want to do that? Just leave us!' And a group of them said, 'Build us a pillar and lift us above it, and give us something to lift our food and drink with so we don't mix with you.' And a group of them said, 'Let us wander the earth and roam and drink like wild beasts. And if you find us in your land, kill us.' And a group of them said, 'Build us houses in the wilderness, and we will dig wells and grow plants, so we don't mix with you nor pass by you.' And there was no tribe member but he had a loved one from them. And God revealed, *'And monasticism that We did not command, but they invented to please God with. Yet they did not observe it as it should be observed'* (57:27). Then others said, 'We will worship as so and so has worshipped, and wander as so and so has wandered, and take houses as so and so has taken houses,' except they were on disbelief, without knowledge of the belief of those they emulated. So when God sent Prophet Muhammad, peace and blessings be upon him, only few of them remained. So the hermit came down from his hermitage, and the wanderer stopped his wandering, and the one in the monastery came out from it and followed him and believed him. Then God, the Blessed and Most High, said, '*O you who believe, fear God and believe in His messenger, He will then give you a double potion of His mercy*' (57:28)-two rewards for their belief in Jesus and the Torah and the Gospel, and following Muhammad and believing him-'*and give you light by which you can walk*'-it is the Quran and following the prophet-'*So that the people of the scripture*'-who imitate you-'*may know that they have no control over God's favor, and that His favor is in His Hand to give it to whomever He wills. And God is the Owner of great bounty*' (57:29)."[44]

- The clash between the political authorities and religion is at the heart of this saying. The kings changed the Torah and Gospel, and demanded that everyone follow them in reading and observing the altered books, yet the faithful refused and remained true to the unaltered books of God. The threat of execution drove the faithful into the wilderness and outside any realm of influence. And so, true faith was restricted to few remote quarters, and disbelief spread in the land.

- The Quranic verse *'And those who do not rule by what God has revealed are indeed the disbelievers,'* was present in meaning or verbatim in the unaltered books. The kings were not applying the revealed laws of God, and their sensitivity towards this verse is clear.

- The origin of monasticism is revealed here as an escape to preserve the purity of the faith. But the trappings of monasticisms were what attracted followers to it, while the creed of the founders was lost; the followers kept the wandering and seclusion without understanding its motivation. The Quranic verses at the end of this saying are directed towards the followers so they recognize the true creed of the founders and stop imitating inherited traditions that have no connection to God.

- God did not ordain monasticism, but people invented it as a vehicle to please Him, and yet they failed to observe it. And with time, monasticism skewed more and more from God's laws and developed errant practices, such as celibacy and flagellation. But God warns against extremism, *"O People of the Book, do not go to extremes in your religion and do not say about God except the truth"* (4:171). The prophets of God are sent as examples, and the Quran states that they had wives and children, *"And We sent messengers before you (O Muhammad), and gave them wives and children"* (13:38). This balance between religious and worldly duties is what God loves and commands.

- The message of Islam restored the true message of Jesus, and found followers among the alienated faithful. Those who embraced Islam from the Christians and Jews received double the reward for believing in and following two prophets of God. This generous reward from God also highlights the difficulty that the faithful might find breaking away from their religious communities and inherited customs. One of the most common obstacles against following the truth is imitation of family and community, and fear of the unknown. Stepping outside the familiar to follow the truth is a mark of courage and piety.

- *"And when it is said to them, 'Follow what God has revealed,' they say, 'We will follow instead what we found our parents doing.' Would they do so even if their parents did not understand, and were not guided!"* (2:170). Some reject the truth after it has become clear because they believe that the ones they imitate must know what they don't, and thus they will blindly follow their choices. But will they do so even when they *know* that they are wrong, and should the truth to be rejected because of the stature of those who choose not to follow it? And now after the truth has become clear to you and you find that they have no support for their claims, will you continue to reject the truth?

[1] *Muslim: The Book of Virtues*, chapter "The Virtues of Jesus, peace be upon him" (6284), Saheeh al-Jaame' (4517).
[2] Bukhaari (3286), Muslim (6282), Saheeh al-Jaame' (5785; 4516).
[3] Saheeh al-Tirmithi (2863), Saheeh al-Jaame' (1724).
[4] Bukhaari (3366), Saheeh al-Jaame' (2579).
[5] Muslim (6286), Saheeh al-Jaame' (3450).
[6] Saheeh al-Jaame' (1497)
[7] Bukhaari (349), Muslim (433), Saheeh al-Jaame' (4199).
[8] Muslim (429).
[9] Muslim (448), Saheeh al-Jaame' (5135).
[10] Bukhaari (3244).
[11] Bukhaari, (3439; 3440), Muslim (443; 447). Al-Nawawi states that both eyes of the Impostor are defective. The right eye is flat with his face and its light is extinguished, while the left is the protruding one.
[12] Bukhaari (7131; 7408), Muslim (2933).
[13] Saheeh Abu Dawood (4320).
[14] Bukhaari (3438).
[15] Muslim (7214).
[16] Tirmithi (2233), Saheeh al-Jaame' (7077).
[17] Al-Silsilah al-Saheehah (2182), Abu Dawood (4324).
[18] Muslim, (7299), Saheeh al-Tirmithi (2240).
[19] Muslim (7568).
[20] Muslim (552).
[21] Saheeh al-Jaame' (4012).
[22] Saheeh al-Jaame' (3919).
[23] Muslim (3089).
[24] Muslim (438).
[25] Saheeh al-Tirmithi (2434; 3148), Saheeh al-Jaame' (8026), Saheeh al-Targheeb (3641).

[26] Bukhaari (7410), Saheeh al-Jaame' (8026).
[27] Bukhaari (3358).
[28] Mukhtasar al-Olo' (69).
[29] Saheeh al-Tirmithi (3062).
[30] Saheeh al-Jaame' (3328).
[31] Saheeh al-Tirmithi (3873).
[32] Saheeh al-Jaame' (3181).
[33] Saheeh al-Jaame' (6292).
[34] Saheeh al-Tirmithi (3801).
[35] Saheeh al-Targheeb (2475).
[36] Bukhaari (3445).
[37] Bukhaari (3435), Muslim (149).
[38] Saheeh al-Jaame' (1463), Al-Silsilah al-Saheehah (1546).
[39] Saheeh al-Jaame' (224).
[40] Al-Silsilah al-Saheehah (2308).
[41] Bukhaari (3446).
[42] Mishkaat al-Masaabeeh (118), with a hasan chain to Obay ibn Ka'b.
[43] Commentary of Ibn Katheer, under verse (4:157). He declared the chain to be authentic to Ibn Abbaas.
[44] Saheeh al-Nasaa'e (5414), with a saheeh chain to Ibn Abbaas.

Glossary

Day of Judgment: The day when people will be resurrected from the grave for accountability before God, then sent to Heaven or Hell. It is also called the Last Day, the Day of Resurrection, and the Hour.

Hadeeth: The sayings and actions of Prophet Muhammad.

Hajj: The Muslim pilgrimage to Mecca.

Islam: To surrender and submit to God. This is the religion of all the prophets of God, from Adam to Muhammad, peace be upon them.

Ka'bah: The cubic structure in Mecca, the site of the first place of worship on earth.

Mosque or **Masjid**: Literally the place of prostration. It is the name given to the Muslim place of worship.

Muhammad: Prophet of Islam and the last of all the prophets.

Muslim: The one who accepts Islam.

Prophet: One who receives revelation from God through Angel Gabriel.

Quran: The Muslim scripture and the Word of God revealed to Prophet Muhammad.

Ramadan: The Muslim month of fasting.